Homeschool Mom Looking Back

Victories & Regrets: Wisdom & Encouragement

DebbieAnn Lewis

© Copyright DebbieAnn Lewis 2024

All rights reserved.

The content within this book may not be reproduced, duplicated or transmitted without direct written permission from the author or the publisher.

Under no circumstances will any blame or legal responsibility be held against the publisher, or author, for any damages, reparation, or monetary loss due to the information contained within this book. Either directly or indirectly. You are responsible for your own choices, actions, and results.

Legal Notice:

This book is copyright protected. This book is only for personal use. You cannot amend, distribute, sell, use, quote or paraphrase any part, of the content within this book, without the consent of the author or publisher.

Disclaimer

Notice: Please note the information contained within this document is for educational and entertainment purposes only. All effort has been expended to present accurate, up-to-date, and reliable, complete information. No warranties of any kind are declared or implied. Readers acknowledge that the author is not engaging in the rendering of legal, financial, medical or professional advice. The content within this book has been derived from various sources. Please consult a licensed professional before attempting any techniques outlined in this book.

By reading this document, the reader agrees that under no circumstances is the author responsible for any losses, direct or indirect, which are incurred as a result of the use of the information contained within this document, including, but not limited to, — errors, omissions, or inaccuracies.

TABLE OF CONTENTS

I can do all things through Christ who gives me strength.

-Philippians 4:13

INTRODUCTION

Well, this is how it all began; I was a working mom. My job was intense, I was always on call day and night. My job was a General Manager of a retail business that was a 24 hour business, always open, we never closed, my employees worked around the clock. Consequently, there were always issues, like covering shifts, handling problems and such. I had 4 children, 2 were already in high school and 2 in the toddler pre-k ages, when I came home for the first time as a stay at home mom. You might be thinking what I was thinking! I had missed out on the day to day time with my older children. They experienced before school after school care, and summers as latchkey kids. They did get to come to work with me as preteens and experience retail and learned a lot of skills that benefited them in such a way, that today they have been able to apply it to their schooling as well as their jobs as professionals and in their own homes with their own children today. Yes, I have been a grandmother for 18 years now. My grandchildren's ages range from 18 years old to 9 years old. When the opportunity came about, that I could come home, not having to work anymore, I was ecstatic, because I had wanted to do that for so long, knowing I was missing out on the most precious years of my kids life. So for the first time ever, not being sick myself or another person sick in the family, I was home for the very first time. Now what to do, I have two little ones, Pre-K age, looking at me to figure out what we are going to do today. It's amazing it can be a terrifying job to be in charge of two young ones and not have anyone else to put the blame on for whatever happens for them and their future. With much prayer, I began to play learning games with my boys. It was simple math games and phonics games and right before my very eyes they were getting it. It was so exciting to see their little lights come on and realize the new things that they were learning and I got to be a part of it. I had experienced this in my working years many times in my job, even daily and in work related things as I was doing training of new employees, teaching others how to do certain tasks and how to be better at their jobs. However, I had not gotten to experience this on a day to day basis with young ones. My time at home in my working years was so busy doing my own chores on nights and weekends that I didn't really focus on anything like this before with my young children. Then I began to read books to understand more of what I was getting into as a homeschool mom and the "how to's"of homeschooling. Then I realized that I have been teaching them all along, because I taught them how to use a spoon, how to tie their shoes, when to be quiet, and taught them how to pronounce words, what colors were what, what shapes are what, I showed them, in growing up. Like, what the words were for what they saw like animals, their sounds and names, stars and airplanes in the sky. It's endless when you think about it.

That is how my homeschooling journey began, 24 years ago. Now looking back, I will share with you my victories and my regrets.

What I experienced; looking back I gained deep and lasting relationships with my boys, that I could never have gotten, had I not spent all the years with them through their homeschooling of elementary and junior high into high school.

The privilege I was blessed with is astounding, that I count as my greatest treasure, my children.

Isaiah 41:10 Do not fear for I am with you;
do not be dismayed, for I am your God. I will
strengthen you and help you; I will uphold
you with my righteous right hand.

CHAPTER 1

MY VICTORIES; WHAT I DID RIGHT!

What I did right, well from the very start I committed myself to the task of focusing on teaching my children. I began the journey slowly, as I had begun playing math and phonics games that my husband, after hearing an ad on the radio as tutoring tools for children, ordered them for us. The boys were learning quickly and liked it, we were doing it together and they liked that. My husband said to me, I think we really need to homeschool the boys. We prayed about it, I did with great fear, I didn't have the faintest idea what or how to homeschool. As for the phonics game, thankfully I had been taught phonics when I was growing up in school and it was way easier to understand than I had first thought it would be, because I already was reading everything that I read myself in a phonetical way. The days went by fast in the very early years as I was getting organized and into the new life I had in now being a homemaker and a homeschool mom. I joined a bible study to learn how to be a homemaker and in that study there were several ladies that were homeschooling as well. I had great examples to look to for advice, for help, veterans of homeschooling that had been doing it for years and raised children as homeschoolers. I didn't realize the privilege of the wisdom that was given to me through those ladies, those incredible moms, that love their children, like no else could. That in itself was a great reason to make this work as a homeschool mom, because I had seen how difficult some years were for my older children as they went through grade school, junior high and high school. There were semesters and years of difficult teachers that had favorites. Teachers who bent to certain ideals that counteracted our family values. It was a great opportunity for us to be able to counsel and educate our children as to why we have the belief, the ideals, and values that we put on ourselves, our family, and our friends. When you can use the examples in real life to show the truth of your own convictions that makes it more real and able to be duplicated in your children. Lots of things we teach our children are because of our own experiences, things that are positive and things that are negative responses and how to overcome those ideals and values as we train our children.

I asked a lot of questions to all of these other veteran moms, the moms that were new to homeschooling as well. I joined co-op groups, to be with other women that were learning alongside me while our kids played at the park, took PE classes, did art classes and had recess play time together. Those were incredible days to hear others were where I was in my journey as a homeschool mom. The support of others around you gives you courage and faith to be able to take the next step in the journey of unknown territory such as teaching our own children reading, writing, arithmetic, art, physical education, history, writing, communication, skills. We all needed these subjects to make us functionable, efficient adults, and good workers for the future career that we chose.

CHAPTER 2

MY VICTORIES; THAT IMPACTED MY KIDS!

My children did not know they were being homeschooled. They were young, they did not know that they were in a different place than most children in the world around us. We had lots of friends, we had lots of activities outside of our home, we had a schedule, we had a start time and for the most part an end time of the day. On the remaining part of the day we would do activities that were learning opportunities as well as the workbooks, bible, math, reading and games. One of my favorite memories and the boys remember well is that Friday was game day. We did not do our regular schedule but it was all about the games. Games are a great way to learn memorization. Looking back I think we learned more on game days because it was relaxed, it was fun and it was sneaky, because the learning was actually not pressured or forced but done through a fun activity, in a competitive way of wanting to win a game that pushed them to learn more about reading and more about getting math figured out. Everyone did their best to use the opportunity to try to win. It brought together the competitive spirit that they needed for their future as men of courage and faith, both in winning and losing skills and fortitude to lead their own families. My goal was to raise young men that love God and love people, and to make disciples of their families first and then others as they can influence them into growing into finer people.

We were working outside the box of a traditional school day that would be sitting at a desk for endless hours with lots of workbooks and textbooks, we did a lot of homeschool hands-on activities. We did not just read about the topic, but we actually experienced the topic. An example of those learning opportunities was going to the lake to learn about hydrology and limnology, and how deep the lake was by sounding, actually getting in a boat (we had to blow it up, first, that's a whole other story) and measuring it.

We went to the river to see how the river flows and the feeling of the water, learning about why the water was so cold and where that runoff was coming from when it was so hot outside. What we were experiencing grew into expanded lessons as we got to see a lot of little river creatures, all kinds of bugs, the occasional snake, I was not too thrilled about that part. We put our hands on everything that we possibly could in each outing experience, sometimes making it happen. I think it's the best way to remember things, the best form of learning that we experienced for ourselves when we can actually walk it, touch it, smell it, feel it, and breathe it in, that's what makes it more enjoyable.

We made lots of dioramas, salt dough creations, and paper mache models of different objects or subjects that we were studying. We made race cars, and derby cars, we had competitions with those race cars and those derby cars as to how they were constructed and the best way to make them faster. Hopefully faster than the others so that you could win first prize. In our co-ops we reenacted history lessons as we learned about the Redcoats, the Boston Tea Party, the Civil War, etc. using pool noodles for swords and battle gear, and as much as we could we dressed the parts too.

I remember the co-op where we were all learning about the history of the United States of America. We got the largest paint tarp from the store we could find. This tarp was so big we almost didn't have enough room in our rented library room. The kids drew the lines, measuring it precisely, as they drew in the lines for each state, they drew in mountain ranges and rivers and lakes, adding the bodies of water to the big map. When we dug deeper we learned about all the states and what they were famous for, like the Big Apple, the Sunshine State, etc. also their state seals, state birds, state flowers, their produce and their commerce. I bought apples of all kinds so that we could have a variety to experience and we blindfolded everyone to see if they could tell which apple was which and which ones they liked the best. That was cool for myself as well because I cannot say that I have ever tasted or been adventurous in the different apple varieties. California is known for its wine. So we bought a whole bunch of grapes and a big cooler bucket that the kids could jump into and actually squish grapes with their feet. Showing them once upon a time how people made wine and grape juice. I think that's probably one of the most memorable pieces in our minds as we think of feet-on not just hands-on, haha!

CHAPTER 3

MY REGRETS, WHAT I WISH I DID!

Looking back at my regrets and what I wish I had done is enjoy it more, not sweat the hard stuff, not worry, not compare, and realize it all works out, in the end. As I am at the end of all of it for 10 years now, I look back and wish that I had enjoyed some of the day to day stuff that seemed like menial tasks and so repetitive but yet the time goes by so fast when you are in it. They say "the days are long, but the years are short!" Some of the menial tasks of the day to day discipline, instruction, is all intertwined into the learning as a homeschool mom teaching her children. You are raising a fine young person to be able to navigate the big bad world that we know they will face on their own someday. I wish there was a future barometer to measure as I went along to assure myself that I was doing well, my kids were going to do great in their future, because of the training we were doing in our daily routine. I am so proud of them and today I realize that in spite of me, they turned out to be terrific adults. They are well rounded, kind, persistent, consistent, strong in their convictions, and steady young men.

If you have more than one child you know this to be true, what works for one kid doesn't or isn't the same for the next kid. My regret would be sometimes putting that pressure on or making the other child perform at a level that the previous one did because of excelling in certain areas. I wish I had realized some of that in the very early years and been more confident to trust that it would work out even if they didn't get some of the essentials that we have in our mind or were even taught ourselves. Some of those skills come by just experiencing them on your own as needed. My younger son was not fond of writing or spelling and saw it as a great chore. He didn't really fight it, he just didn't really have interest in it because it was boring as such. So timing is everything, it became a big deal to him when he got his first phone and got to texting with his friends that he realized the importance of spelling things correctly and having good grammar, to make sense of what he was trying to say. There's nothing like peer pressure to push the truth quickly like that did for him. It just wasn't natural that he was interested in pursuing the spelling before that moment.

Comparing is one of the most dangerous things we can do to our kids whether you are a homeschool mom or just a regular mom or dad. Each one is fearfully and wonderfully made, created just the way he or she was supposed to be, to become a person to add value to the rest of the family in a unique way that could only be done if they are who they are, not someone that we force them to become.

The influences around you are sometimes part of the regrets realizing that we pick up attitudes, thoughts and actions of others and place them as value on our own kids by forcing them to comply because another mother said this was valued and her kids as being superior than mine because of it and you look at your kid and think that they should do it as well. I regret getting caught in that loop a few times because I was succumbing to the peer pressure of the other mothers that were around me. They were telling me how great their kids were. I then questioned myself and my ability as to whether my kids were as good or could be as good, thinking that I was failing them as their homeschool teacher because I was not seeing the same achievements that the other moms were bragging about in their kids. I regret not taking action sooner and leaving that co-op group that was toxic to me and to my kids, sooner. We had spent a year and a half with that group. It was a learning lesson for all of us and learning more about people and just because they are in the same kind of learning opportunities and church does not mean they hold the same values that we hold. It helped us all to use it as a teaching tool of how to recognize behaviors and attitudes that are not beneficial for us.

My regrets would be how much value I put in some other mothers' opinions. Other homeschool moms were there for both support and challenging me to be a better teacher, the regret side how I compared my kids to theirs. How I felt like I didn't measure up or that my kids were falling behind. Some because they wanted to be super moms, you know the kind; the one upper kind, the kind that belittles you because of her own pride and then consequently I find that I myself was doing the same thing that I despised in them. Then others were true and genuine moms who really saw the potential and were rooting for my kids to do great along with theirs. It's important to keep a self check and make sure that you are truly there for your kids and not your own pride.

With prayer and seeking guidance from The Lord to equip you to do the best for your kids. You are their mom because you are the best choice for that person to grow under your leadership, your love now and forever.

One of my regrets would be to realize that it really truly does all work out in the end. Whether they were at public school or a private school or even homeschooled, what we absorb as children makes us who we are as adults. Some of the influences and experiences we have in our life make up who we are in a good way and also in a bad way. I was in private school for all of grade school and in public school for high school and college. I know the influences of that protection of private school and the leniency of the public school developed in me certain opinions and added to my ability to get along in the real world. Some of the worries about how much we progressed in learning in our studies were more important in their college studies, learning as it fit to the degrees that they received. It happened because they were interested in a certain topic and it became a reality to be successful and to graduate with that degree. In the right time they were able to focus on that area of possible weakness, it truly does all work out, just as it did for you and me.

My regret is, how fast it goes. Some days time stood still, they were hard days. Days that no one wanted to work, including me. Some days were time out days that we all needed to go to our own corners and just have some peace. I regret as I wish I could have not gotten caught up in some of those days in my head about, "oh no we're not getting it done", or "oh no, I'll be behind now". "oh I won't get all the pages finished in this book before we are ending our school year for a summer break". As my kids are now approaching their 30s no one has lost sleep about a workbook page that is blank or a book not finished, or a historical gap in the timeline, or the ones I was always going to get done. That's the regret, is that I wish I could have known more of that trusting that it would all work out. I wasn't failing, neither were my kids. We built something so much better, we have solid relationships with each other, my boys are each other's best friends. That is the reward of the steady plodding of the everyday grind we did together. We made memories, we grew together. We experienced life together.

My regret is not doing more pajama days or free days. Also, not doing more hands-on days, more trips and we did a lot but yet those were the fun days and the building memory days, the ones we talk about now and the ones that we remember and treasure as the good days of homeschooling. I am not saying that you should be all fun and no work but in the fun times we learned a lot about others and about ourselves. My regret would be that I wish that I had realized I was going to learn a lot and I didn't have to know it all before we got there, as a family, as a homeschool mom and her kids, that's why I say I wish that I had not sweated the hard stuff and not worried.

It's really easy to get caught up in the rat race of, "would of, should have, could have" and not enjoy the journey, the successes and the victories. It's the same with life, "Right?" We all have that and you can do that also as a homeschool mom and have it out for your kids and not really build a relationship that lasts. At the very least make the kind of relationship that you want to have, that they bring their family over to your house, just because they really want to see you and they want to share with you all the things that are happening in their life. That's the goal; that's the reason that we give up our time, our career, our money, promotion opportunities in our best years, our best earning years, it's for these that I love so much. It's easy to get caught up in the rat race of success, of the world's standards of achievement, it's destructive and hurtful more than it could ever be helpful or positive. What does it profit a man to gain the whole world and forfeit his soul, or be rich with no family around!

My personal regret would be not truly believing I could teach my own children and that I was capable and competent even though it was new territory for me. I was not trained as a teacher specifically. I had one family member that was dead set to say that I had no business being their homeschool teacher because I did not have a degree in teaching as she did. Although she had her own teaching degree, she would not even tutor her own children but certainly was okay teaching other people's children. Beware of those around you that want to steal the joy of homeschooling. That was bothersome for me, it brought about doubt a lot of times and I regret that I could not shake her words against me, allowing doubt to creep in on me.

One thing that helped me overcome some of that doubt was that I was thankful for the answer sheet. It was definitely my backup and the assurance of the teaching that I was on the right track and that it was in black and white, how hard can that be, but I did like to challenge myself to stay sharp in my mind about the subject and get my own answers to the questions before looking up the answers as well. Maybe that was my coping with staying with subjects that seemed trivial but necessary for the boys to learn and keep my presence and with the repetitive nature, it took to get those basics nailed down. Everyone has to start somewhere and having the patience to do that sometimes is the challenge, that regret would be finding the patience that I did not have on some days or some subjects or with some needed stamina for pushback from one of the guys. It's funny how they are little humans with thoughts and feelings and stubbornness in areas that they don't care for and the conflict that we can get into with them over it. I regret not understanding that fully and getting myself caught up in the battle with the little guy as he did not want to do the work that I felt was essential to be completed. I know that's part of being a parent first but it does overflow into homeschooling as their teacher and instructor and over looming fear of not doing enough, always questioning myself, am I failing them or helping them?

CHAPTER 4

MY VICTORIES AND GOOD DECISIONS!

Co-op opportunities were to grow all of us, with out of the box experiences that influenced me and my kids. We had both good and bad in those, some were so fun, we forgot that we were there to learn because it was so fun and a natural learning experience. We looked so forward to being with them every week, the kids with the kids and the moms with the moms and all of us together learning. I grew as a teacher, as an educator and the kids grew to love learning, we found it could be fun and that the world was interesting, it was all available for us to explore. The best part is whatever piqued our interest we could pursue, we didn't have to stop because the class period was over or there was no more information in the textbooks or workbooks. Whatever the subject that we were working on, if it was boring or not fulfilling and not keeping the kids interested then we can move on and do something else. Using different ideas, topics that had their interest, proved to be the best and deepest of their experiences. That was the amazing part to be able to run with a topic until we exhausted ourselves or got bored with it and then on to the next subject, or challenge that came our way, we were flexible to things that were happening around us, things that are happening on the news, world events, things like elections, weather, anomalies in the sky, learning about animals because of a zoo visit or something we saw on the hike or an outing. The ability to be able to pursue learning in tactile-like projects, that really kept the boys interested in learning and exploring new things. I found the boys were less likely to want to sit at a desk and hold a pencil. We were able to enjoy the exploring side of their desires deep within them. As a rule, I find the girls are more likely to be able to sit still longer. It's funny I didn't even realize that I knew this from being in school myself as I remember the nuns taking a ruler to the boys for not paying attention or for not being able to sit still in their seats. Maybe that's why the girls were better at sitting still because we had fear of that happening to us. Funny how you remember certain things as you experience them later in your life as a flashback of a time and a place. Isn't that what we are hoping to get out of our schooling time together, was to have reflections later about an event or timeline that we had experienced as kids that was positive and even being able to use the negative opportunities as learning tools for the future. I am thankful for the time that we were able to pursue the tactile-like projects and physically challenging endeavors for the boys sake and for learning sake, that would be one of my victories.

Certainly, one of the victories that I feel I got a good handle on early on was to keep the boys physically active, like between penmanship, workbook pages and math sheets. One of the fun things they will tell you they remember well was finishing a workbook page or a set of math problems, so they could do their LeapFrogs, or Jumping Jacks and tumbles up and down the hallway on the hot days and on the beautiful weather days we had a trampoline out back, that they could go out and jump around and just use up some energy, after that they could focus again on the work we had before us. I loved the days when we brought our books outside on the trampoline. We could just bounce about a little bit.

It was those close times when we started reading a story and we were all snuggled up together involved in the story waiting to find out what would happen next. Each story we read had some kind of learning, like about how to be a good person, make good choices, and an adventure that we could learn from. That's the fun of reading and learning new things. As a mama, I will always treasure those times together, the days that I will never have again, like that, of those little ones in my arms.

CHAPTER 5

ME, LOOKING BACK!

Looking back, I realized the impact of being with them day to day, it added confidence, safety, assurance, true love, for the future well being of great little humans who will serve well, respect others, excel in their careers, and truly be great men.

The victory as I see now in my children, they are confident. They hold themselves well; they do not have fear of forging ahead in their careers, advancing to the next levels and pursuing that next promotion.

As for safety, others are safe around them. They are confident in handling their own bodies, being able to temper another person's anger by being able to handle themselves or providing protection for someone else in need. One of the best things that we invested in was to put them through karate classes. They spent 6 years in karate. We attended most weeks at least three times a week. We had a great instructor, an honorable sensei. He was well respected in our community and his program was top-notch. The boys learned respect from him and his teachings. We were teaching that at home as well but it is always great to have that area reinforced. It's great that it can be displayed and taught as a backup to prove as good reasons to pursue honor and integrity as a lifestyle. No one has ever said that people had too much respect or too much honor in their character, sadly it's the opposite that there was no respect and had no honor for others.

As for assurance, we did things like oral book reports with our co-op friends and families. Practicing speaking before others is a great quality to have to be able to use for future jobs. People that speak before others are well respected. They hold themselves with confident assurance that makes the audience comfortable and able to understand them better. Along that same line we did stuff like Toastmasters to practice the next level of speaking before others, being able to stand up and deliver a speech or to be able to speak publicly took them to the next level.

Sports were a big part of confidence builders in our boys. They played baseball from pee wee league to travel ball and into high school and on to college. That was a blessing that they pursued baseball and loved it. They were also good at it which helped in the scholarship area of paying for college. Being a team player is a very important skill to learn, it is one that continues to pay well in adulthood because we all have to get along with others and then be able to use it in their own families.

Also, in those confidence building years we did gymnastics with our homeschool friends during the day, before the other kids were out of school. It provided a great opportunity for smaller classes. It also worked into our day as PE classes. The instructors worked them hard and they were very sweaty and enjoyed every second of it.

Other years we did PE classes at the park with our larger Co-op groups. While the kids were enjoying time with the coaches and playing games and exercising, the moms were together exercising our experiences, our trials and learning new things from each other. It was great that some of the veteran homeschool moms would lead the discussions or do a skill lesson for us as beginners or intermediate homeschool moms, depending on the ages that we had in our current families. I learned a lot from those veteran moms that gave of themselves and their time to us other mothers as we were learning to be homeschool instructors and teachers. Now, as I am discipling younger women these days, I see the reward that they received for giving of themselves to us. Those park days were awesome to be a part of, to learn from, to build our confidence and for the task before us to teach our children. They talked about different curriculums that they liked and were successful with and helped formulate ideas on how to capture our kids' attention and desire for learning. Some of the ladies that I sat with in those days are still some of the friends I have today because of the time that we spent together at the park days.

My victories were to follow along with opportunities and try everything we could do to have the boys have a well-rounded experience of different activities. One of those activities was to be involved in drama. There was a homeschool drama group that we joined for them to be able to do acting, with parts in plays and performances. They both had a desire to do drama in high school, which was a huge confidence builder for them to be able to perform in front of others.

CONCLUSION

In conclusion, my victories and what I did right, I stayed committed, I prayed, I asked questions, and I asked others for help when needed. I relied on my husband for support, to be a sounding board, to coach me to stay in the battlefield of homeschooling, to celebrate my victories with me and to help me with my defeats and my regrets along with my victories. The truth is my husband and I were in this together although I was in direct charge of the day-to-day homeschooling, while he was at work, he was my support. He was the one cheering me on knowing that this was the best that we could offer to our children. It was because of him and his encouragement that I pursued homeschooling our children. I could not have done it without his support and his encouragement.

I was hard on myself and he continued to keep my feet on the ground about it being the best thing, the best way for us to grow our boys into good strong men that love God, love people, and could make disciples of their families. The impact, and the discipline of continuing the day-to-day sometimes grinds on but having another day was a privilege and a blessing that I could never truly grasp until it was finished. I can now look back and see the deep and lasting relationships I have with my boys because of the time we spent together.

In my victories and regrets, I ponder so many things as I have those days now behind me. I know I cannot change one of those days, I can only do something with today. So today I offer to you my experiences as encouragement and wisdom, "What I wish I knew", "What I wish I had done", "What I wish I had done more of". I do not regret homeschooling my boys. I wish that I could have homeschooled all four of my children. I love them all equally for each has their own individual talents that are precious to each of them.

They are mine and I love them with my whole heart and would give anything for them, if it were at all possible.

The greatest thing about a mother's love, is that I love them like no one else can, I am their only mother, no one can take my place or be me in their life. You can't beat a mother's love, "Mama Bear and all".

My children are forever in my heart. I have a unique bond with my children that I homeschooled. I think I had a great advantage that in my early years for my first couple of children I was a working mom, maybe that's the reason I treasured the latter two of them so much and I was able to treasure homeschooling and be their mom-teacher. I knew what it was like to miss out on the day-to-day learning, the excitement and experiences that I only got to hear about. It was a privilege to be able to experience the day-to-day with my boys. I am so proud of them all, those raised with me looking in from afar and those whose direct daily influence I got to be a part of in the day-to-day of their growing up years!

EPILOGUE

Some verses that we live by:

Proverbs 5:21 For the ways of a man are before the eyes of the Lord and He watches all his paths.

Proverbs 6:20-23 My son, observe the commandment of your father and do not forsake the teaching of your mother; bind them continually on your heart and tie them around your neck. when you walk about they will guide you; when you sleep they will watch over you; and when you wake, they will talk to you. For the commandment is a lamp and the teaching is light; and reproofs for discipline are the way of life.

<u>Proverbs 22:6</u> Train up a child in the way he should go and when he is old he will not depart from it.

<u>Proverbs 1:7-8</u> The fear of the Lord is the beginning of knowledge, fools despise wisdom and instruction. Hear, my son, your father's instruction and do not forsake your mother's teaching

<u>Lamentations 3:22-23</u> The steadfast love of the Lord never ceases; His mercies never come to an end; they are new every morning; great is Your faithfulness.

Matthew 6:33-34 But seek first His kingdom and His righteousness, and all these things will be added to you, therefore do not worry about tomorrow, for tomorrow will worry about itself. Each day has enough trouble of its own.

Philippians 4:6-7 Do not be anxious about anything but in every situation, by prayer and petition, with thanksgiving present your requests to God and the peace of God, which transcends all understanding, will guard your hearts and your minds in Christ Jesus.

1 Peter 5:2-3 Be shepherds of God's flock that is under your care, watching over them- not because you must, but because you are willing, as God wants you to be; not pursuing dishonest gain, but eager to serve; not lording it over those and trusted to you, but being examples to the flock.

Psalms 127:3-5 Children are a heritage from The Lord, offspring a reward from Him. Like arrows in the hands of a warrior are children born in one's youth. Blessed is the man whose quiver is full of them. They will not be put to shame when they contend with their opponents in court.

2 Timothy 3:14-16 But as for you, continue what you have learned and have become convinced of, because you know those from whom you learned it, and how from infancy you have known the holy scriptures, which are able to make you wise for salvation through faith in Christ Jesus. All scripture is God breathe and is useful for teaching, rebuking, correcting and training in righteousness

Deuteronomy 6:6-9 These commandments I give you today are to be on your hearts. Impress them on your children. Talk about them when you sit at home and when you walk along the road, when you lie down and when you get up. Tie them as symbols on your hands and bind them on your foreheads. Write them on the door frames of your houses and on your gates.

Ephesians 6:1-4 Children, obey your parents in the Lord, for this is right. Honor your father and mother which is the first commandment with the promise so that it may go well with you and that you may enjoy a long life on the earth. Fathers, do not exasperate your children instead bring them up in the training and instruction of the Lord.

www.ingramcontent.com/pod-product-compliance
Lightning Source LLC
Chambersburg PA
CBHW071953120726
48001CB00005B/2160